Greetings From
Rutland, Vermont

Heart of the Green Mountains

Debby DuBay

Schiffer Publishing Ltd

4880 Lower Valley Road, Atglen Pennsylvania 19310

CENTRAL RANGE OF THE GREEN MOUNTAINS

Rutland, Vt.

Title page: Center Street looking west. Fabulous mountain views, charming shops and galleries and special events such as the Friday Night Lives (held every Friday evening through-out the summer) make Rutland a must to visit.

Schiffer Books are available at special discounts for bulk purchases for sales promotions or premiums. Special editions, including personalized covers, corporate imprints, and excerpts can be created in large quantities for special needs. For more information contact the publisher:

Schiffer Publishing Ltd.
4880 Lower Valley Road
Atglen, PA 19310
Phone: (610) 593-1777;
Fax: (610) 593-2002
E-mail: Info@schifferbooks.com

Designed by Stephanie Daugherty
Type set in Times New Roman/Staccato222 BT/Times New Roman
ISBN: 978-0-7643-3730-7
Printed in China

For the largest selection of fine reference books on this and related subjects, please visit our website at **www.schifferbooks.com** We are always looking for people to write books on new and related subjects. If you have an idea for a book please contact us at the above address.

This book may be purchased from the publisher. Include $5.00 for shipping. Please try your bookstore first. You may write for a free catalog.

In Europe, Schiffer books are distributed by

Bushwood Books
6 Marksbury Ave.
Kew Gardens
Surrey TW9 4JF England
Phone: 44 (0) 20 8392 8585; Fax: 44 (0) 20 8392 9876
E-mail: info@bushwoodbooks.co.uk
Website: www.bushwoodbooks.co.uk

Dedication

This book is dedicated to the Rutland Free Library, Rutland Historical Society, Paramount Theater and Rutland Mental Health - with all royalties from the book being donated to these not-for-profit agencies. To Edward M. Godnick, a veteran and entrepreneur who believed Rutland was a great city and to Steve Eddy - Rutland's best friend!

Acknowledgments

This book is a culmination of data regarding a community that started when James Mead arrived in 1769. Rutland is a place of pride. It is a town with salt-of-the-earth people who love their families and appreciate nature and the environment—people with strong work-and-play- hard ethics. In 2007 it was that type of people I met when I first arrived, with my successful antique business of fifteen years, to downtown Rutland. Without the support of this community, this historic and retrospective book using antique post cards would not be possible. The news printed in local papers and magazines (special thanks) stated that "a new person in town was looking for antique postcards for a book!" With that request, people stepped forward.

Specific thanks go to Patricia Kreitzer formerly of the Creative Economy, the Downtown Rutland Partnership Director Michael Coppinger and his assistant, Don Wickman; to my fellow colleague Mary Fran Lloyd; to my dear friends Director of the Killington Music Festival Maria Fish and Attorney-at-Law Judy Barone—whose father Edward M. Godnick passed away during my research; and to my assistant Rachael Barbagello for her professionalism and support.

Sincere appreciation goes to Stephen Smith, owner, of Foundation Antiques, 148 North Main Street, Fair Haven, Vermont. An avid postcard collector, expert and historian, Steve happily provided me with most of the color postcards and all but one of the rare black and white photograph postcards used in this book. Without his contribution this book would have not been possible. For further information on historical post cards or to purchase any of the postcards used in this book, contact Steve at his email: foundationantiq@hotmail.com.

Special thanks also go to Problem Solver Tom Lichtman, from Vtweb.com; to Paul Gallo and Peter Miller who graciously donated many personal family post cards; Ryan Gallagher who donated four post cards from his private collection; Anthony and Carnie Albarello, Virginia Crete, Mary Crowley, Casey "Jim" Diamond, Helen and Jim Davidson, Henry Duval, Bob Ferron, Debbie Kirby, Joan Korda, Martha Goodwin, Tom Giffin, Ryan Gallagher, Phil and Britney Matte, Nick Nikolaidis, Penny Inglee, Tim at Timco Gallery, and Steve Smith for providing me with information and allowing me to use their postcards.

Also thanks to historian Don Wickman for his assistance in editing and for the use of his list "from A to Z" of some of the famous, locally-grown Rutlanders.

All my love and appreciation to my family who support and believe in me. My mom, Charlotte Klassy DuBay, for doing my research and for being my personal editor. To my dad for making us laugh, to my sister Lori DuBay LaBarre for providing technical support and for managing my website; and my brothers, Mike and Dave, one the rock the other the hammer. To Feli, Robert, Bradley, Jerry, Alisha and Nicole—"the DuBay family." To my mother-in-law, Yolanda Quinn, my friend and the mother of my husband, Dan Quinn.

Also to my dog family in Tinmouth, Vermont, at North Star Dog Training School: Carolyn Fuhrer, Kathy Duhnoski and pack, Pam Badger and Pheobe, Winnie Denis and Hagred, Sue Engle and Magic, Annie Glendenning, Max and Olivia, Doris Ingram and Sadi, Debbie Granquist and Ellie, Kellie Morrison and Olive, MiMi Neff, Keeta and Lily, Debbie Peretz and Mollie, Jenny Server and Clemmy, Karen Svenningsen and Dreamer, Rene Traverse and Brewski, Kappi and Sherlock, Gretchen and Chewey, Brenda and Blossom and Jane, Sam and Charlie! I could not have survived without you. And to my Standard Poodles, Paul and Lincoln, who I love with all my heart!

Contents

BIRD'S EYE VIEW OF CITY FROM PINE HILL, RUTLAND, VT.

Bird's Eye View of City from Pine Hill, Rutland, VT. C.T. American Art. $7-8

1

Welcome to Rutland

Rutland, Vermont — located in the heart of the Green Mountains on Otter Creek—has picturesque vistas that are postcard perfect! Rutland is in a valley that was formed by the Green and Taconic Mountains. Rutland is the second largest metro area in Vermont. Although, when ranked by population—according to the 2010 census—Rutland's population is 16,495 and is technically the fourth largest city in Vermont. (Burlington, approximately sixty-eight miles north of Rutland, is the largest city in Vermont with a population of 42,417, South Burlington has a population of 17,904. Essex approximately seventy-five miles north has a population of 19, 587 and Colchester comes in third with 17, 067.) Montpelier, the capital of Vermont, is located sixty-seven miles northeast of Rutland, with a population of approximately 8,000. Based on the 2010 census, the total population of Vermont is 625,741. With an estimated dairy cow population of 154,000, the myth has been dispelled that Vermont has more dairy cows than people!) Rutland is nowhere near the two major Interstate Highways 89 and 91, but is considered the "Crossroads of Vermont" by Vermont tourism because the city is intersected by U.S. Routes 4 and 7. The result: Rutland has kept its quintessential Vermont charm, a "support Vermont first" attitude, and a salt-of-the-earth community.

Rutland—*connected naturally*—is the home of the largest Farmers' Market in the state and the only Winter Farmers' Market. Rutland Farmer's Market is open from May to October every Saturday and Tuesday at Depot Park in Downtown and every Saturday during the winter at the Co-op, Downtown on Wales Street. You will find products produced by local farmers: fruits, vegetables, eggs, cheese, maple syrup, honey, baked goods, preserves, plants, cut flowers and artisan-made handcrafts and original art.

Rutland is led by an energetic mayor who is assisted by organizations such as the Creative Economy with the Arts & Culture, Open Air, Recreation and

Greetings From Rutland Vermont. Vermont is called the Green Mountain State with Rutland being in the heart of the Green Mountains. Montpelier is the capital, Burlington and South Burlington are the largest cities in the state, followed by Rutland. Linen post card published by Norcross-Eldridge Co., Rutland, Vt.. $3-4

Sustainable Rutland committees, all working to make Rutland a more vital and vibrant community through creative thinking and initiatives. Rutland is home to the beautiful Chaffee Art Center, located on Main Street in a magnificent old mansion. It is a Vermont art gallery and cultural center holding regular shows and openings.

Heart of Rutland (Heart opens to display 12 miniature post cards: Rutland Rail, Memorial Hall, Berwick House, Masonic Temple, Memorial Library, etc.). Shown is St. Peter's Church, High School, and 1st Baptist Church. Hand-made from a black and white photo, copyrighted 1907 by Glazier Art Co., Boston, MA. Cancelled Jan. 3, 1908. $15

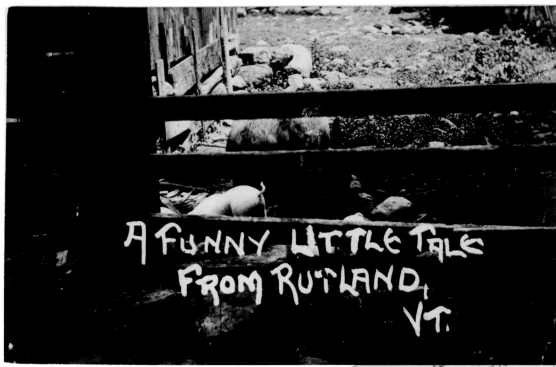

A Funny Little Tale From Rutland, VT. Black and white Photo
Post Card. Genuine Photograph made by "The Art Store"
Winsted, Ct. Cancelled July 20, 1909. $35

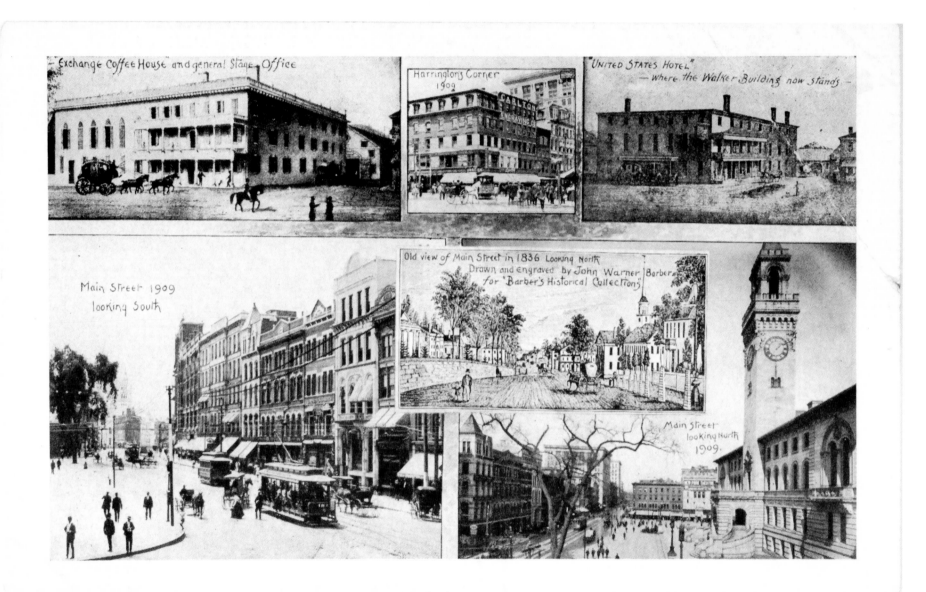

1909 Rutland, Vermont post card showing Coffee House, Harrington's Corner, United States Hotel and Maine Street views. Published by William A. Emerson, Worcester, MA. Torn edge effects value. $3-4

Genuine black and white photo post card of Rutland, VT.
Cancelled 17 May, 1912. $25.00

Greetings From Rutland, Vermont.
Lindholm's Diner "Good food and friendly
service day and night" US Highway signs
for Route 4 and Route 7. Rutland is at the
intersections of US Rts 7 and 4. $15-18

Greetings from Rutland, Vermont

Rutland, Vt.. Central View of the Green Mountains. Enjoy panoramic views and vistas while visiting Rutland. Original photograph post card. Cancelled Jun. 12, 1907. $15-18

Thanks to the leadership, energy, and enthusiasm of the Downtown Rutland Partnership, Rutland's Downtown is the center of activity with unique characteristics that include the Friday Night Live concert series from June to August and "Art Hops" held the second Friday of every month throughout the year. "Shop, eat and be entertained " is the motto of Rutland's charming Downtown. Downtown Rutland has antique shops, art galleries, a book store, toy store, bakery, florist, furniture store, food stores, jewelers, clothing stores, restaurants, night spots, a farmer's market, dance studios, wellness center, salons, performing arts center and great events. (For further information visit: www.rutlanddowtown.com)

The Paramount Theater, located on Center Street, is one of the most beautiful classical theaters in New England. It is the only fully restored National Landmark presenting theatre between Burlington, Vermont, and Pittsfield, Massachusetts. It was opened in 1914 by George Chaffee as the Playhouse Theatre, but the name was changed to the Paramount Theatre in the 1930s. The theatre was saved in the late 1980s by a heroic community effort, restored to its former glory and reopened in 2000. Dazzling world-class entertainment, from concerts by John Hiatt and Bela Fleck, productions of Hamlet, to entertainment by Jungle Jack Hanna and Garrison Keillor, are what have become expected, thanks to the leadership of the board and executive director. (For further information visit www.paramountvt.org or www.paramountlive.org.) The Paramount Theater also hosts groups such as the Rutland Youth Theater, a "for the kids" program supported by Rutland Recreation and Parks Department.

Bird's Eye View, Rutland, Vermont 66. Fairchild Aerial Surveys, Inc., taken for the Rutland News Co., Rutland, Vt.. "C.T. Art-Colortone" post card. $7-8

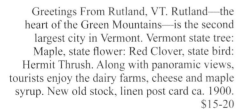

Greetings From Rutland, VT. Rutland—the heart of the Green Mountains—is the second largest city in Vermont. Vermont state tree: Maple, state flower: Red Clover, state bird: Hermit Thrush. Along with panoramic views, tourists enjoy the dairy farms, cheese and maple syrup. New old stock, linen post card ca. 1900. $15-20

Unique and charming colored post card from an era gone. "I wish you were in Rutland, Vt.. To Help Me Steer Around The Town." On the back it is addressed to "Master Vern Newton" reads: "Hello Vern how be you— well I hope-—suppose you go to school every day don't you wish I was with you we would have some fun would we not—I guess we would—be a good boy until I come, Ma" "c/o Mrs. D. Wyman." Cancelled Oct.. 3, 1913. $15

Vermont, birds eye view Rutland.
$4-5

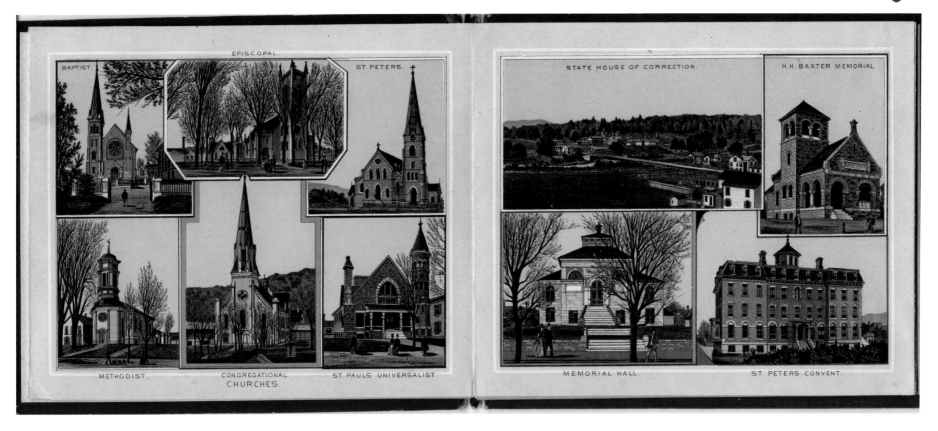

BAPTIST. EPISCOPAL. ST. PETERS. METHODIST. CONGREGATIONAL. ST. PAULS UNIVERSALIST. CHURCHES.

STATE HOUSE OF CORRECTION. H.H. BAXTER MEMORIAL. MEMORIAL HALL. ST PETERS CONVENT.

Anthony Marro:

After starting his journalism career at the *Rutland Herald*, Marro worked for the *New York Times*, *Newsweek* and *Newsday*, the last sixteen years as its editor.

Mary McGarry Morris:

Raised in Rutland and a graduate of Mount Saint Joseph, Morris is an acclaimed novelist. A writer of seven books, several have been made into movies and one title, *Songs in Ordinary Time*, was a *New York Times* best seller.

William T. Nichols:

This Civil War veteran served in the 1st Vermont Regiment and then commanded the 14th Vermont Regiment at Gettysburg. After the war he survived the sinking of the S.S. Republic in 1865, made several successful business ventures and in 1869 with several other Vermonters founded the village of Maywood, Illinois.

Robert Pierpoint:

A successful Rutland attorney, Pierpoint served as Vermont Lieutenant Governor during 1848-1849.

Arlie Pond:

Pond was a pitcher from 1895-1899 in the National League and then enjoyed a noteworthy career in medicine, first in the Army and then assisting the people of the Philippines.

Edward Hastings Ripley:

At age twenty-two Ripley became a captain in the 9th Vermont Regiment when the regiment formed in 1862. During a sixty-three day period in 1863 Ripley received promotions to Major, Lieutenant Colonel and Colonel. By August 1864 he attained the rank of Brigadier General at age twenty-four. On April 3, 1865 he led the first Union brigade into the Confederate capital of Richmond, Virginia.

TOWN HALL.

COUNTY COURT HOUSE.

POST OFFICE AND U.S. COURT HOUSE.

MRS. J. B. PAGE.

C. P. HARRIS.

H. H. BAXTER.

MRS. J. C. R. DORR "THE MAPLES."

PRIVATE RESIDENCES.

William Y. W. Ripley:

The older brother of Edward Ripley, this Ripley also served in the Civil War. He first captained a company in the 1st Vermont Regiment and then gained the rank of Lieutenant Colonel in the elite 1st United States Sharpshooters. At the Battle of Malvern Hill on July 1, 1862 he performed gallantly and for his actions, earned the Medal of Honor.

George Schmitt:

A pioneer in the early stages of aviation, the twenty-one-year-old Schmitt was tragically killed in a flying accident at the Vermont State Fair in 1913.

Charles Sheldon:

Greatly influenced the creation of Alaska's Denali National Park.

Israel Smith:

The versatile Smith was a four-term member of the U.S. House, a U.S. Senator, Vermont Chief Justice and governor.

Robert T. Stafford:

Serving first as Vermont's Attorney General, lieutenant governor and governor, Stafford went on to be elected five times to the U.S. House of Representatives. After being appointed to fill a vacancy in the U.S. Senate, he served another seventeen years in that body. The Robert T. Stafford Student Loan program is named in his honor.

Frederick Dorr Steele:

Grandson of Julia Dorr, Steele was a talented illustrator, providing artwork for books by Twain and Kipling among others. He is best known for his drawings of Sherlock Holmes, taking Arthur Conan Doyle's character and adding the curved Calabash pipe and deerstalker hat.

Wheelock Veazey:

Veazey was in the Third and Sixteenth Vermont Regiments and for his actions at the Battle of Gettysburg on July 3, 1863, subsequently awarded the Medal of Honor. From 1890-1891 he was the Commander-in Chief of

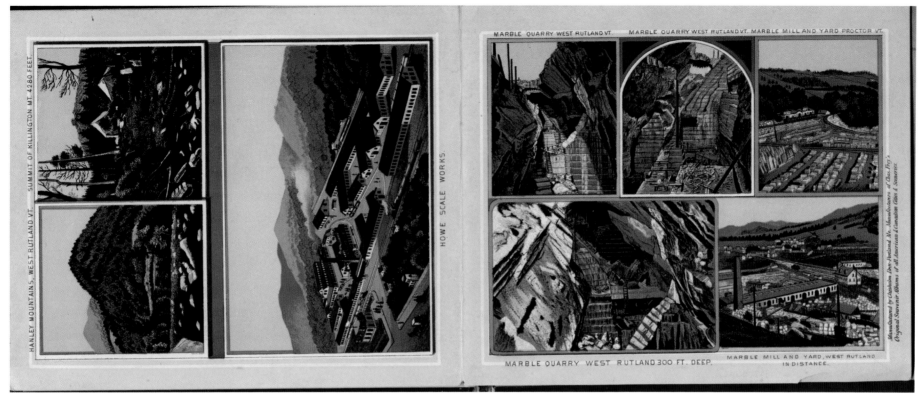

the veterans organization the Grand Army of the Republic. He served as a member of the Interstate Commerce Commission in the 1890s.

Aldace F. Walker:

Joining the 1st Vermont Heavy Artillery at age twenty-two, Walker rose to the rank of lieutenant colonel by war's end. He commenced a respectable law career until being appointed to the Interstate Commerce Commission. He resigned that post to work for the Sante Fe Railroad, becoming its president and then chairman of the board.

Samuel Williams:

Besides being the first minister of the East Parish Congregational Church (now Grace Church) and a cofounder of the *Rutland Herald*, Williams composed in 1794 the first published history of Vermont; *The Natural and Civil History of Vermont*.

Leonard Wing:

A graduate of Norwich University and self-read for law, Wing dedicated himself to the military. He enlisted during World War I and shortly thereafter joined the Vermont National Guard. Wing rose to the rank of Brigadier General. His guard unit was activated in 1941 and during the war in the Pacific he became commander of the 43rd Division with a rank of Major General.

Steve Wisniewski:

n All-American offensive guard at Penn State, Wisniewski subsequently played thirteen seasons for the Oakland Raiders. He participated in eight Pro Bowls and gain selection to the NFL 1990s All-Decade Team.

In addition, former Vermont governors from Rutland were: Israel Smith, Charles K. Williams, John Page, John Mead, Percival Clement, Charles Smith and Robert Stafford. Rutland has many other noteworthy Americans that are not recognized by name in this book. Their contributions have been as leaders, activists, aviators, artists, athletes, business owners, conservationists, entrepreneurs, farmers, inventors, war heroes, patriots, writers, poets, presidents, public servants and good people—proudly Rutland has produced them all!

Rail trestle above Meads Falls, Rutland, Vt.. James Mead was Rutland's first settler arriving at these falls on Otter Creek in 1769.
Mead built his saw and grist mills on the falls.

2

History & Industry

MARBLE YARD AT WEST RUTLAND, VT.

Marble Yard At West Rutland, Vt.. Quarrying grew rapidly in West Rutland and became the primary source for block marble for the Vt.. Marble Company. Tracks were used to move the marble. Note St. Bridget's Catholic Church in background. It has been said that the marble worker's life was work, church and family. $3-4

Rutland was settled in 1770 and incorporated as Vermont's third city in 1892. Rutland is sometimes called "Home of the Marble Men" because the settlers in and around Rutland depended on quarrying to make a living. In the 1830s a large deposit of nearly solid marble was found in what is now West Rutland but the quarries did not prove profitable until 1851 after the railroad arrived. As luck had it, the famous quarries of Carrara in Tuscany, Italy grew unworkable, allowing Rutland Vermont to become one of the world's leading marble producers. This fueled growth and investment and in 1886 the center of town was incorporated as Rutland village. Most of the town became West Rutland and Proctor because they contained the bulk of the marble quarries.

In the Fall of 1849 the Rutland and Whitehall Railroad was opened. This line connected Rutland's marble to a port on the Champlain Canal solving the problem of hauling marble thus opening up new markets for Rutland marble. By 1860 the rail industry was supporting thirty-three companies.

Marble Valley, Rutland, Vt.. Note the railroad cars in the background. The Clarendon and Pittsford Railroad was organized to serve the marble industry. "Rutland is the center of the marble interest of Vt.. It is a region rich in limestone and marble has been quarried here since 1830. Population about 15,000." Post card ca. 1908. $7-8

A Vermont Marble Quarry, Rutland, Vt.. The quarries grew deeper and larger as the Vermont Marble Co. extracted more and more marble. Power tools increased the efficiency of the process. Photo ca. 1894. Cancelled Nov.. 24, 1908. $7-8

Marble Valley, showing Engine House and Derrick, Rutland, VT. $7-8

Traveling Crane, Center Rutland, Vt.

Traveling Crane, Center Rutland, Vt.. Cancelled Mar 31, 1907. $8-9

Rutland, Vt., Railroad Station

Rutland, Vt.. Railroad Station. $12

Railroad Station, Rutland, Vt.

Rutland, Vt.. Railroad Station. At the turn of the century Rutland Railroad Station was the center of activity and was the spring board for a developing downtown. $15

Mid Century black and white photograph of Rutland Railroad Engine Number 100. $19

Rutland 81. Rutland Pacific, built in 1925 in Schenectady, New York; in Rutland, Vermont, Jan. 8, 1950. Everything in this photo is now gone and replaced with a shopping center. $9

Mid Century black and white photograph of Rutland Railroad. $10

Rare black and white photograph post card of Rutland, Railroad Station. Sent from Mrs. Webster 138 ½ West St., Rutland to Mr. Chandler of Hubbardton, Vt.. Cancelled May 26, 1909. $50-60

Rare black and white photograph post card "President Coolidge (30th President of USA) visiting Rutland Aug. 3-'23". Coolidge was born and is buried in Plymouth Notch, Vermont. Perfect condition. $30-40

Depot Square, Rutland, Vt.. Cancelled Aug.. 18, 1933. $7-8

Early 20th Century black and white photograph of post card of Depot Square. $20

20th Century post card of Depot Square, Rutland, Vt.. "Rutland, Vermont. Vermont's second largest city is the 'hub' of the Green Mountain State centrally located on U.S. Rts. 7 & 4. It is a trade as well as a recreation center, ranging from industrial production to tourist attractions." Photographed by Frank L. Forward. Pub by Forward's Productions, Manchester, Vt.. $3-4

Summit, Vt.. Highway Bridge over Big Cut on line of Rutland Railroad. Cancelled at East Wallingford Post Office May 14, illegible year. Ca. 1900 $15

Vermont Cavendish Gorge, Rutland R.R. Cancelled Jul. 17, 1907.

10263 Center Rutland Falls, Rutland, Vt.. Detroit Publishing. Late 19th Century view of an early steam engine heading west over a steel bridge that crossed the Center Rutland Falls. $7-8

10263   CENTER RUTLAND FALLS RUTLAND VT

Otter Creek, Rutland R.R. Vt.. $3-4

Otter Creek, Rutland R.R. Vt.

Redfield Proctor mansion. In pristine condition, currently serves as a single family home.

This solid marble bridge was built over the Otter Creek falls, in Proctor, Vt.. A major passageway for Native Americans. Previously there had been three wooden bridges (1794, 1811, 1839) over the 123-foot falls. Built in 1915 by the Vermont Marble Company, the Marble Arch Bridge replaced the last covered bridge. Restored in 2002 and given as a memorial to Fletcher D. Proctor from his mother Emily Dutton Proctor.

Proctor cemetery looking toward Saint Dominic's Catholic Church. The church and head stones are made of local marble.

The Proctor family mausoleum in the Proctor cemetery, Proctor, Vt..

View of marble church and mountain vistas.

Saint Dominic's Catholic Church, South Street (Rt 3) Proctor built in 1926 from local marble. The original Saint Dominic's was built in 1880 and used through 1926.

Marble Street Historic Building in Downtown West Rutland, owned by the Rutland Community Land Trust & Merchants Bank. Managed by and home to Glen Campbell's fabulous marble studio "The Carving Studio & Sculpture Center Gallery".

West Rutland High School made from local marble.

Building on Merchants Row in Downtown Rutland. This building, currently home of Citi-Smith Barney and offices, is included on the Rutland marble trail because it is decorated with local marble.

Gawet Marble and Granite Company located on Business Rt 4. Established 1919, offers local marble and granite and the restoration of both.

OMYA entrance sign made from local marble. Global producers of industrial minerals.

During the 19th Century local marble was used for not only buildings and bridges but for foundations, walkways, walls—if it could be made out of marble it was!

RAILS & SCALES

Rutland Railroad

The Rutland Railroad was a small railroad primarily in the state of Vermont and extending into the state of New York. Chartered in 1843 by the state of Vermont— the Rutland and Burlington Railroad Company became the hub of many intersecting railroads. The Clarendon and Pittsford Railroad was organized to serve the marble industry in the area. By 1867 the Rutland and Burlington Railroad had changed its name to simply Rutland Railroad. The Railroad allowed transportation of Rutland's booming marble industry from the Great Lakes to the ocean. In addition it serviced the Howe Scale Company located right along the Rutland Railroad line.

Between 1871 and 1896, the Rutland Railroad was leased to the Central Vermont regaining its independence when the Central Vermont Railroad entered receivership. The New York Central Railroad briefly had a controlling interest in the Rutland Railroad from 1904 through the next seven years. In 1911 the New York Central Railroad sold half of its shares to the New York, New Haven and Hartford Railroad. The Rutland Railroad entered receivership for the first time in 1938. Struggling financially, a reorganization in 1950 changed the name from Rutland Railroad to Rutland Railway.

21st Century photograph of Rutland Railroad Station. The former Depot Square now the parking lot for the train, Community College of Vermont and shopping center that includes Wal-Mart, TJ Max, etc.

Friends of Rutland Rail

In January of 2009, in response to Vermont Administrative proposals to end Ethan Allen service in an attempt to adjust the state budget, the Friends of Rutland Rail was founded by Herb & Roberto Font-Russell. In an effort to save the train, hundreds of friends, members of the community, local Vermont legislators, city officials and Rutland Regional Chamber held rallies at the Jim Jeffords Amtrak Station. In addition, over one hundred supporters made a trip to a legislative hearing in Montpelier. These actions brought attention to state government, the Governor backed down and the train was saved.

The effort continues as the Friends of Rutland Rail promote the building of Vermont's Western Rail Corridor with returning passenger service from Bennington to Burlington. The organization continues to have positive results in Rutland: with beautification of the station; convincing Amtrak officials to place new signage and information venues for the public; assisting with the reopening of Amtrak at Castleton Station in January of 2010; and each Spring celebrating National Train Day.

The Vermont Rail Action Network (VRAN) has partnered with the Friends of Rutland Rail to expand and promote updated rail service. VRAN named Herb Font-Russell to its board in 2009 and awarded him the Herb Ogden Vermont Rail Activist Award at their annual dinner. These organizations—along with the Rutland Railroad Association of Center Rutland—are attempting to continue the long established proud history Rutland has played on the national rail scene as home to the Rutland Railroad.

Today, because of the hard work and dedication of many including Christopher Parker, Executive Director of Vermont Rail Action Network; Tom Donahue, Executive Director Rutland Region Chamber of Commerce; and the *Rutland Herald*, Rutland is the terminal for Amtrak's Ethan Allen Express providing daily service to and from New York City. **"RUTLAND"** is proudly displayed as a destination on Penn Station's big schedule board in New York City! (For further information, contact the Vermont Rail Action Network at 1-800-USA-RAIL or visit: www.railvermont.org)

Howe Scale Company

The history of the Howe Scale Company begins with Frank M. Strong and his friend, Thomas Ross of Vergennes, Vermont, who designed and patented a ball bearing scale for the Sampson Scale Company of Vergennes. Their invention assured the scale rests would not become worn down. This ball-bearing design provided a shock absorber for the pivot, reducing stress and assuring scale accuracy. Strong and Ross are credited with this first major scale improvement in America, along with inventing a gigantic scale for weighing canal boats in 1857.[7]

21st Century photograph of the Howe Center Business Park, 1 Scale Street sign.

21st Century photograph of the Howe Center. Lovingly restored by the Giancola family while maintaining the integrity of this historic building.

In the spring of 1864 John Howe Jr. of Brandon, Vermont, purchased Strong and Ross' patents and began to manufacture scales as the Howe Scale Company. The Howe Scale Company became world-renowned, earning several awards at fairs and exhibitions, including the gold, silver, and bronze medals at the 1867 Paris Exhibition.

In 1872, Howe Scale's Brandon plant was damaged by fire. Looking for a new location—and based on the fact that the rail was required in distribution of the Howe Scales—in 1873 Howe Scale moved to Rutland. John A. Mead of Rutland became the president in 1886, followed by Carl B. Hinsman and Frank G. Riehl. The Howe Scale Company went on to manufacture the weightograph, a device which produces weight readings on a ground glass screen that can be read in the dark from some distance away. It also produced the longest railroad track scale in the world, scales for weighing airplane propellers, and lightweight, aluminum scales that were easily transportable on airplanes. It also began producing trucks and trailers for cargo, an important part of the company's product line. The Howe Scale Company continued to be a leader in the manufacturer of high-accuracy weighing instruments into the twentieth century. Unfortunately the plant closed in 1982.

The efforts of Joe and Barbara Giancola in restoring the Howe Center, and his sister Angie, who brought Rutland together with the new Franklin Community Center, Rutland has begun a new phase of prosperity. The Giancola's renovations

21st Century photograph of the Howe Center old scale yard. After a fire gave the Brandon site cause to move, the train was the reason for the Howe Center's move to downtown Rutland.

OMYA train runs on the rail track in front of the Howe Center. OMYA is a major employer in the Rutland area and Vermont. Founded in 1884 by Gottfried Plass-Stanfer in Offringen, Switzerland.

include utilizing the existing buildings while maintaining the historic charm. Slate roofs were repaired and window panes replaced. The buildings were brought up to code and each tenant had a space built to their specific needs and requirements. The "Howe (Giancola) Building" no longer houses scale production, but is a center where many forums take place and a variety of businesses are housed, such as Westminster Crackers (established in 1828), Harte's Floors, Historical Pages Printing Company and K9 to 5 Dog Training.

DAIRY

Along with marble and freight service, Rutland Railroad also served the dairy industry. At one time called the "Million Dollar Train" Rutland's industry and milk train made up the significant portion of the Rutland Railroad's profits.

Every state in the United States has dairy farms, but warmer climates are not conducive to year-round milk production. Approximately 88 percent of milk produced in the United States comes from the 22 states considered to be the nation's "Dairy Belt," which extends from New York to Minnesota. Wisconsin, "The Dairy State," is the second largest dairy-producing state with California (no where near the Diary Belt) producing the most milk in the country. California

has surpassed Wisconsin in total dairy production since 1994 and has held the lead ever since. For 1997 and 1998, California produced 7.1 billion pounds of milk during the April-June quarter (the season of highest milk production), while Wisconsin produced 5.8 billion. Other leading dairy states are New York, Pennsylvania, and Minnesota.

Thomas Dairy is a small, family-owned dairy nestled in the beautiful, rolling hills of central Vermont. In 1854, when Orin Thomas purchased a farm of approximately 325 acres, it is unlikely that he knew he was beginning a family business that would continue to grow and prosper over the next three generations. In 1901, Orin Thomas bought his first purebred Holstein cow. In 1909, at the time of his death, his son, Orin Jr., took over management of the farm and its forty purebred Holsteins. In 1921, Orin Jr. started [8] delivering milk (for 11 cents a quart) in Rutland City, and Thomas Dairy was born.

Dairy farming continues to be a major industry in Vermont. Since the mid-1940s, the number of dairy farms has steadily decreased to approximately 1,500 farms today, each having an average of seventy cows. Taking advantage of the latest technology, total milk production per cow is at an all-time high, yet larger dairy farms weaken the ability of small and medium farms to compete. In Vermont, farmers sell their milk to member-owned dairy cooperatives that process and distribute milk and other dairy products. Vermont's emphasis on *"buying and supporting local,"* along with Farmer's Markets and tourists, are marketing tools for the family farms.

MAPLE SYRUP

Most dairy farmers produce cheese (Vermont is famous for the "World's Best Cheddar" at the Cabot Creamery) and maple syrup. In the past, syrup makers were self-sufficient dairy farmers who made both syrup and sugar for their own use and for extra income. By tapping Black and Sugar Maple trees, farmers collected their sap in the spring.

The sap-collection process continued to evolve as a result of innovations in their work. In 1864, a Canadian man borrowed some design ideas from sorghum evaporators and put a series of baffles in flat pans to channel boiling sap. In 1872 a Vermonter developed an evaporator with two pans and a metal arch, or firebox, which greatly decreased boiling time. Seventeen years later, in 1889, another Canadian bent the tin that formed the bottom of a pan into a series of flues, which increased the heated surface area of the pan and once more decreased boiling time.

The technology remained the same until the 1960s, when it was no longer a self-sufficient enterprise with large families as farm hands. Because syrup-making was so labor intensive, farmers could no longer afford to hire large crews

Family-owned and operated Sugar & Spice Restaurant and *Sugar Shack*, on Route 4 toward Killington Ski Resort, is known for their delicious pancakes, authentic Vermont ambience and fantastic maple syrup!

run by the Hathaway family for three generations. Prior to their purchasing the farm in 1942, the Osgood family had owned the farm for five generations. The Osgoods raised potatoes and were known as the Potato Kings of Vermont. They were also one of the largest maple syrup producers in Vermont. Today, the Hathaways raise "all natural beef" and have the largest corn maze in Vermont while they continue to produce Vermont maple syrup.

TOURISM

Tourism is a major industry of Rutland and Vermont. Rutland's location in the foothills of the Green Mountain National Forest provides 400,000 acres of diverse landscape for activities such as hiking, skiing, snow boarding, biking, motorcycle riding, fishing, golfing, apple picking, bird watching, and gondola or sleigh rides. Tourists can shop, find antiques and frequent one of the many marble exhibits and art galleries, including the Norman Rockwell Museum of Vermont, the Maple Museum and the Chaffee Art Gallery on Main Street. Since 1914, the Paramount Theater, on Center Street, has entertained visitors who can stay at a romantic inn or the Killington or Pico Ski Resorts. Alpaca farms and wine tours are also nearby, making Rutland a popular destination for all who visit Vermont!

to gather the buckets and haul the sap to the evaporator house. During an energy crunch in the 1970s, syrup makers responded with another surge of technological breakthroughs. Tubing systems, which had been experimented with since the early part of the century, were perfected and the sap came directly from the tree to the evaporator house. Vacuum pumps were added to the tubing systems. Pre-heaters were developed to recycle heat lost in the steam. Reverse-osmosis machines were developed to take a portion of water out of the sap before it was boiled. Several producers even obtained surplus desalinization machines from the U.S. Navy and used them to take a portion of water out of the sap prior to boiling.

The technological developments continue today. Improvements in tubing, use of vacuums, new filtering techniques, "supercharged" pre-heaters, and better storage containers have been developed. Research continues on pest control and improved woodlot management. In 2009, researchers at the University of Vermont unveiled a new type of tap, which prevents a back-flow of sap into the tree, reducing bacterial contamination and preventing the tree from attempting to heal the bore hole.

Many local farmers produce maple syrup and sell their bottles at gift shops, the Farmer's Market or at their own farm stands. The 1881 Hathaway Farm, now on the National Historic Registry of Historic Places, has been owned and

The historic 1881 Hathaway Farm Barn. A generational family farm known for all-natural beef, the largest corn maze in Vermont and fine Vermont maple syrup.

11290 MERCHANTS' ROW, RUTLAND, VT.

Merchants Row looking south. The Morse Block was purchased by the Rutland Savings Bank in the 1880s. Right, is the ornate tower of Baxter National Bank. First town hall at the site of City Hall juts into view at the far end of the street. Note the main line rail car stopped in front of the passenger station at 51 Merchants Row. $7-8

3

Downtown: Attractions, and Celebrations

Since the arrival of the railroad, Downtown Rutland has been the center of the town's activities. Merchants Row has historically been the heart of the shopping area. In the late nineteenth century, it was suggested by the Rutland Board of Trade that the name Merchants Row be changed to Broadway, but it never happened. Depot Park, the Rutland Railroad Station and street car stops made Merchants Row the major north-south street while Center Street runs east-west. Historically, Center Street has been the shopping district of the city and is also noted for restaurants and the Paramount Theater.

Today, Rutland's Downtown has unique characteristics, such as the Friday Night Live concert series from June to August, and "Art Hops," held the second Friday of every month throughout the year. Downtown Rutland has antique shops—including the world-class Limoges Antiques Shop[9], art galleries, a book store, New England's best toy store (Michael's Toys), a bakery, a florist, a furniture store, food stores, jewelers, clothing stores, restaurants, night spots, Vermont's best year-round farmer's market, dance studios, a wellness center, salons, performing arts center and great events. The Rutland Food Co-op is member-owned with locally grown and produced products. The Paramount provides world-class entertainment for all who love fine music, plays and entertainment. (Visit www.rutlanddowtown.com)

The Rutland Playhouse opened in 1914 and was one of the finest theatres in New England, designed with ornate detailing, frieze, hand carved moldings and cornices, hand painted ceilings and lush draperies. In the 1930s it was renamed the Paramount. By the mid twentieth century it was in dyer need of repairs. Thanks to a group of dedicated benefactors, funds were raised and the Paramount was renovated in 1980. Today, the Paramount offers second-floor art space as the Bagley Lobby and the Brick Box, that host exhibits and openings for unique artisans and crafters.

Rutland is also home to the largest Halloween parade in the United States, thanks to Tom Fagan. In 1960 Fagan, a local writer and comic book fan, influenced friends, fellow authors and comic book fans to participate in the Rutland Halloween parade. By 1965 Fagan had character costumes to include Batman, the Joker, Plastic Man, and Dr. Strange. Every year more comic book heroes appeared. In 2009 Rutland celebrated the Halloween parade's fiftieth anniversary with thousands of spectators enjoying floats with themes that ranged from "Hair" to "Grease". Sadly, Tom Fagan passed away on October 21, 2008, but his love of comic book characters remain in his legacy in the Rutland Halloween parade.

Rutland, Vt.. Depot and Merchants Row. Note the Rutland Street Railway Company car. Cancelled Oct.. 1911. $7-8

OLD RUTLAND, 1855, MERCHANTS ROW
B. M. BAILEY, SILVERSMITH

Clement Bank, Rutland, Vt.. On the corner of Merchants Row going north—currently the site of the TD Bank. This post card is from "Lila" 58 N. Main St. Rutland, Vt.. Cancelled Oct.. 26, 1905. $7-8

Old Rutland, 1855, Merchants Row, B.M. Bailey Silversmith. $7-8

Black and white photograph post card of early Merchants Row looking North. $35-40

1950s "Merchants Row, Rutland, Vermont heart of the shopping area. Photo taken from part of the parking lot" looking north. $3-4

Merchants Row looking north. H&H Clothing Store on the right the Opera House on the left. $3-4

NEW GRYPHON BUILDING, RUTLAND, VT.

LOOKING UP WEST STREET
FROM MERCHANTS ROW – RUTLAND, VERMONT.

Looking up West Street from Merchants Row – Rutland, Vermont. Left is the marble building currently Citizen Bank. Directly across the street is the site (Jun. 2010) of the Rutland Region Chamber of Commerce. $10-15

On the corner of Merchants Row and West Street (Business Rt. 4A) New Gryphon Building, Rutland, Vt.. Here it is "Howley Corner." 21st Century it was the site of several ladies' clothing stores—the most recent "Fruition Fineries." $7-8

21st century Merchants Row looking north. Michael's Toys, Limoges Antiques Shop, The Sandwich Shoppe, Fruition Fineries, Chamber and "The Bun" at the corner of Merchants Row and West Street, Business Route 4; 10,000 cars a day pass through this intersection!

Rutland Restaurant established 1917. Four generations owned by the Anaynos family. Along with the restaurant they cater parties. Home of Burnham Hollow Pies. (Note Champion Ellie Granquist.)

21st Century photograph of the Mead Building at 98 Merchants Row. Home of Clem's Restaurant and coffee shop, 96 Merchants Row - Tattersall's Fun, Funky, Funktional Clothes & Accessories. Next door Three Tomatoes Restaurant. Although ever changing, Rutland City and their Downtown maintain the quintessential charm tourists love.

Wal-Mart and parking lot currently stand in the location of the former Depot Square.

Boys and Girls Club located on Merchants Row, Downtown, Rutland caters to the youth in the region.

Black and white photo post card of the Mead Building (ca. 1940s) showing the corner that wraps around on Center Street. $10

The Mead Building at the corner of Merchants Row and Center Street. Dr. John A. Mead owned the Mead Building and was President of the Howe Scale Co. His building burnt down in 1906 sadly with no insurance. He has a large formal family monument in Evergreen Cemetery. $3-4

The New Mead Building. Cancelled Nov.. 6, 1906. $3-4

Bardwell Hotel, Rutland, Vermont at the corner of Merchants Row and Washington Street. Built in 1852 by Ortis Bardwell and E. Foster Cook. John W. Cramton purchased the building in 1864 and enlarged the Bardwell on the North end. $7-8

Center Street, Rutland, Vermont. Easterly view. Addressed to Whitcourt's, Minneapolis, Minnesota. Cancelled Nov.. 11, 1911. $7-8

Glidden Tour, July 23, 1908 at the Bardwell House, Merchants Row/Strong's Ave, Rutland, Vt.. Tour sponsored by AA (now – American Automobile Association) to create their first road map. $10-12

Center Street, Rutland, VT. Copyright, 1904 Detroit Photographic Co. Tuttle Building (13 Center Street) housed the Rutland Herald and Globe in the 1880s. Tuttle & Co. owned by the Tuttle family was a book, stationery, printing and binding company. Building currently houses Rutland's Book Store. Note the steeples. On the left the Congregational Church on the right the Baptist Church . $7-8

1950s view of Center Street, (looking east) Downtown Rutland. Back of the card states: "Center Street Rutland, Vermont. It is a very busy shopping center where you will find excellent stores to take care of your shopping needs and gifts. Forward photo and production." Note the Berwick Building, a 1973 casualty of fire, in the photo. $3-4

Looking west on Center Street, Rutland, Vt.. "The largest and most important city in the central part of the State. Showing Carroll Cut Rate Store, the largest Drug Store in Rutland." New old stock card ca. 1940/1950. $4-5

Center Street looking east. Steeped in arts and culture, Rutland also has events from bike rides and marathons to autism and breast cancer walks.

Genuine black and white photograph post card of Center Street - Rutland, VT. Note Howe's Coffee Shop - The H. H. Howe Company (21 Center Street) was the center of confectionery goods, ice cream, candies, etc., from the mid 19th into the 20th Century—and Carroll Cut Rate store. Currently Simon the Tanner. $20-25

Mid 20th Century "Partial View of the Business Section of Rutland Vermont." Post card published by Rutland News Co., Inc. $7-8

Center Street, Looking West From Berwick Street, Rutland Vermont. Colored post card cancelled Sept.. 2, 1925. $8-9

The Paramount Theater on Center Street. The Paramount has been lovingly restored to its original grandeur by a group of community volunteers. Vermont is lucky to have one of the most beautiful theaters in New England that hosts world-class performances right here in Downtown Rutland.

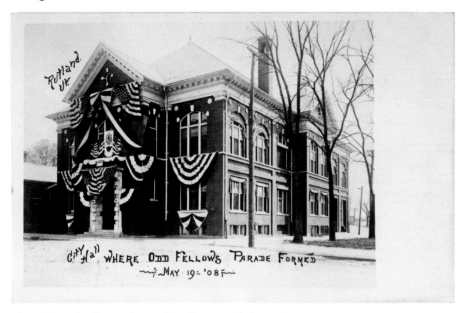

City Hall, Rutland, Vt., where Odd Fellows Parade formed May 19, 1908. Downtown Rutland shopkeepers are historically known for their patriotism and love of parades. Rare black and white photo post card. $35

Metzger Bros., Rutland, Vermont. Building decorated for President William Taft's visit on Oct.. 8, 1912note the viewing box . President Taft gave a two minute speech on the Berwick Hotel's balcony. The original William Metzger Upholstery Shop was established in 1876 on Evelyn Street. In 1901 the shop moved to Center Street into the H.L. Verder Steam Bakery building—currently known as the Metzger Building. Today, home to BROC (Bennington-Rutland Opportunity Council Inc. Community Action Program) the recently refurbished building is diagonally across the street from the "Pit," formerly the Berwick Hotel. Black and white post card vs. photo post card. $15

Center Street - Merchants Carnival, September 5th to 10th, 1910 original black and white photo post card distributed by Clauson Shoe Co., 19 Center St., Rutland, Vt.. "The Place to Buy Your Shoes." During the late 19th and early 20th century downtown celebrated the week of the state fair held at the Rutland Fairgrounds. Today buildings on Center Street remain—the shops have changed: Arts and Antiques on Center Street, The Book King, Back Home Again Restaurant, Gus', etc. $30

Genuine black and white photograph post card of the Berwick on Center Street, Downtown, Rutland, VT. First floor housed retail shops such as the M. Steiner & Sons Piano Shop in 1908. Burned, renovated and named the Town House. Sadly on Jan. 7, 1973 it burned to the ground. Several lives were lost and adjoining buildings were damaged. Cancelled Feb.. 2, 1908 as is condition with ink spot. $25-30

The Berwick Hotel,   Rutland, Vermont.

Early 19th Century post card of the Berwick. The "Town House" Berwick burned to the ground in 1973. Today a parking lot known as the "pit"—currently the site of a redevelopment mixed use project opening in 2011. $8-9

Merchants' Row, Rutland, Vt.

Clement Bank building shown on corner of Merchants Row. Decorated for the Rutland Carnival an event during fair week. Note the awnings, trolley cars and horses in the downtown more than a century ago—the buildings remain the same—store fronts, cars and clothes have changed! Cancelled Sept.. 1, 1906. $20

The Bardwell Hotel on Merchants Row decorated for fair week—the hotel was a terminal for transporting visitors from downtown to the fairgrounds. Note people waiting on porch. Rare black and white photo post card. Corner damage affects value. $35

Rutland community had a fondness for including automobiles in events and parades. Rare black and white photo post card. $40

Rutland community had a fondness for including automobiles in events and parades. Rare black and white photo post card. $40

Car decorated as butterfly wings with children. Rare black and white photo post card. $50

The Playhouse, Rutland Vt.. On Center Street in downtown Rutland, the Playhouse opened in 1914. Rivaling the Wang Theater in Boston, the Rutland Playhouse has ornate detailing, frieze, hand carved moldings and cornices, hand painted ceilings and lush draperies. Photochrom post card. Cancelled Aug.. 12, 1914. $9

Balloon Ascension June 18, 1909 Rutland, Vermont. Rutland gasworks provided heat and lights and gas for enterprising balloonists. Pilot William Van Sleet, Professor W.H. Pickering of Harvard University and J.B. Benton of the Boston Transcript launched into the air and landed in Laconia, NH two hours and fifteen minutes after take-off. A memorable event for the crowds in 1909. $100

The Playhouse, Rutland, Vermont. Thos. A. Boyle, Manager. Today—as magnificent as it was in the 1914s—the Paramount has world class entertainment from Broadway musicals to famous entertainers and international productions. The Paramount has a Board of Directors and is managed by Executive Director Bruce Bouchard. Perfect condition, new old stock. $15

City Hall, Rutland, Vt.. Cancelled Jun. 19, 1912. $5-6

Rutland, Vt.. – Memorial Hall. Memorial Hall of the Grand Army of the Republic constructed in 1883 at 151 West Street. Housed the Rutland Free Library on the lower level until moving to Center and Court Street. Torn down in 1931 replaced by new construction currently housing the United States Post Office and Court House. $3-4

Site of the original Court House built in 1870. Currently the Leonard F. Wing, Jr., Mediation Center.

United States Post Office and Court House, Rutland, Vt.. At 151 West Street former site of Memorial Hall. $3-4

Masonic Temple, Rutland, Vt.

MEMORIAL ARMORY, RUTLAND, VERMONT. 38

Memorial Armory, Rutland, Vermont. Built in 1920 on West Street near the intersection of Main Street (Rt. 7). Home of the Vermont National Guard. Cancelled Jul. 30, 1929. $3-4

Rutland, Vt. Old State House, Built 1775, Where State Legislature met in 1784 and 1786

Masonic Temple, Cottage Street, Rutland, Vt.. Cancelled Jul. 10, 1908. $8-9

Rutland, Vt.. Old State House. Built 1775. State Legislature met in 1784 and 1786. The first U.S. District Court session in Vt.. was held here in May, 1791. This building was torn down in 1912. Cancelled Jul. 1900. $4-5

Savings Bank Building, Rutland, Vermont. Built in 1868; always a bank on the first floor. The Morse Block, corner of Center and Merchants Row, was purchased by the Rutland Savings Bank in the 1880s. Verde marble façade was added in the 20th Century. New old stock. $10

On the corner of Merchants Row and Center Street this building, built in 1868, has always been a bank building. Currently home to Lake Sunapee Bank. Owned by the Foley Family of Companies established in 1879. The Foley motto: "We began Downtown, we're invested in Downtown and we're committed to making our hometown the best it can be!"

21st Century photograph of the Rutland County Court House.

Clement Bank, Rutland, Vermont. At the intersection of Merchants Row, Center and Evelyn Street. Currently Clement Bank/TD Bank. Constructed in 1884 for a cost of $60,000. New old stock. $10

Building on the corner of Merchants Row and Evelyn Street. Formally Clement Bank currently the site of TD Bank. The clock keeps perfect time!

Marble Bank, currently the home of Citizen's Bank, on the corner of West and Merchants Row.

The Rutland County National Bank marble structure 71-77 Merchants Row. Opened by the Ripley family in 1861. $3-4

Interior of Marble Savings Bank, Rutland, Vt.. 45 Merchants Row currently Citizen's Bank. Constructed of locally quarried marble the interior combines marble, wood and tile. New old stock. $8-9

Old Rutland Bank, Rutland, Vt.

Handcolored

Old Rutland (Savings) Bank, Rutland, Vt.. Chartered in Nov.., 1824 as the fourth bank in the state, building complete in June 1825. A consideration in 1970 for Rutland Historical Society. Cancelled Aug.. 23, 1909. $8-9

In the Heart of the Green Mountains   :::   All Summer Sports—Golf, Tennis, Fishing

BROCK HOUSE

Open All Year---Booklet on Request.   H. S. PARKER, Owner, RUTLAND, VERMONT

"In the Heart of the Green Mountains – All Summer Sports – Golf, Tennis, Fishing, Brock House, Open
All Year --- Booklet on Request. H.S. Parker, Owner, Rutland, Vermont." Cancelled Sept.. 21, 1926 $10

5

Street Views

Taking a walking tour of Rutland, or walking along the Rutland portion of the Vermont Marble tour, you come across historic buildings and homes built in the Victorian Queen Anne style (1880-1890). This style is elaborate, yet romantic and feminine, and may be built from brick or stone (in Rutland you will notice the use of marble). This style of home may have towers and spindles with lavish "gingerbread" decorations. One also notices many center-entrance colonial homes distinguished by their elegant entries with simple floor plans and a fireplace or two. In addition, Rutland has many buildings from the late 1700s through 1850, a period associated with the colonial style in the United States. These houses may have a porch and a fireplace, even a turret, depending on the country of their influence.

The influence of the Killington and Pico ski communities has inspired the Ski Chalet or Swiss Cottage style of home in the outskirts of Rutland. This style has large windows and rough-cut lumber with projecting A-frame roofs. Many[10] are of post-and-beam construction. Today there are lovely new areas of 21st century construction, such as those by Gene Hathaway and Dean Davis.

Quigley's House, 88 Center Street, Rutland, Vermont $7-8

Residential Section, Rutland, VT $4-5

Little's Lodge, 92 Center Street, Rutland, Vermont $7-8

LORETTO HOME, RUTLAND, VT.

Loretto Home, Rutland, Vt.. Built in 1903 as the Catholic Old Ladies Home. $7-8

Rare photo post card. Loretto Home, Rutland, Vt.. $15

Garden at the "Maples." Residence of Mrs. J.C.R. Dorr, Rutland, VT $10

The Brock House, Rutland, Vt.. Cancelled Dec.. 15, 1909 $8-9

"The Maples" Residence of Mrs. J.C.R. Dorr, Rutland, VT. Copyright 1904, by Detroit Photographic Co. Julia Caroline Ripley Dorr (1825-1913) spent most of her life in Rutland. Considered one of Vermont's foremost literary figures in poetry. The daughter of William Y. Ripley, Mrs. Dorr was the first president of the Rutland Free Library. She wrote an ode for the opening of the Ripley Opera House in 1868. She lived, wrote and died in the house called "The Maples." $10

Rare black and white photo post card of the Congregational Church, Rutland, Vt., the third structure to house the west parish. Built in 1855 on Pleasant Street in West Rutland. The first Congregational Church is in Rutland Center. East and West split in 1787. Not cancelled $20

21st Century photograph of Grace Congregational Church, United Church of Christ established 1788.

Rutland, Vt.. St. Peter's Church. $7-8

Catholic Church of Christ the King, Rutland, Vermont. On Main Street next to Rutland Mental Health. Colorcraft, published by Norcross-Eldridge Co., Rutland, Vt.. $7-8

Inside of Church, Rutland, VT. Cancelled Jan. 15, 1908. $1

Rare original photograph made into a post card of the First Church of Christ Scientist, Cottage St., Rutland, Vt.. Taken by H. B. Rood Photo, Poultney, Vt.. $15

Black and white photo post card of Evergreen Cemetery. $35

Rare black and white photo post card of Main Street in Center Rutland. Rt 4 currently Business Rt. 4A leading from West Rutland into Rutland City. Note the old store and school both lost in fires Dec.. 20, 1907 and January 10, 1908 respectively. Today it is the site of a convenience gas station. Evergreen Cemetery is across the street. Cancelled Sept.. 15, 1908 prior to the fire(s). $50

James Mead family burial plot in Evergreen Cemetery. James Mead was Rutland's first settler arriving in 1769. He was an ardent defender of the New Hampshire Grants and served as a Colonel in the militia. His descendents have played major roles in the development of Rutland.

Covered in moss, "Christian and Philanthropist" are the two major words inscribed on James Mead's head stone.

Entrance to Evergreen Cemetery, Rutland, Vt.. Colored post card cancelled Mar 1, 1920. $7-8

Entrance to Evergreen Cemetery the oldest cemetery in Rutland.

Vista view of Rutland City from the top of Evergreen Cemetery.

21st Century photograph of the George E. Royce family burial plot in Evergreen Cemetery. The most unique burial sites in Evergreen Cemetery.

Rare black and white photo post card of St. Joseph's Convent of the Sisters of St. Joseph, Rutland, Vt.. Dated Dec.. 25, 1910 script note: "Another New Year my dear boy, I wish you health, I wish you joy, Sincerely, E.A. Fintell." Addressed to Sidney Butterfield Rutland Fire Department (RFD) No 1, Rutland, Vermont. $50

St. Joseph's Convent, Rutland, Vt.. Located on Convent Avenue. In the early twentieth century Convent Avenue was an ethnic and cultural neighborhood in Rutland. On the same street was St. Peter's Church and the Loretto Home. Cancelled Sept.. 4, 1910. $8-9

7

Education

Public schools managed by the Rutland City School District include:

Rutland High School

Rutland Middle School

Rutland Intermediate School

Northwest Primary School

Northeast Primary School

The district also runs the Stafford Technical Center. Private schools include:

Catholic Christ the King School (elementary)

Mount Saint Joseph Academy (secondary)

Rutland Area Christian School

The city is home to two colleges:

College of Saint Joseph in Vermont (formerly College of Saint Joseph the Provider)

Community College of Vermont (CCV)

Church Street, Rutland, Vt.. Public School. The first Rutland High School located in the old Academy building. In 1929 when the new Rutland High School was built on Library Ave this location became the intermediate Meldon School. In 1957 with the building of the new Rutland Jr. High the Meldon School was abandoned. In 1969 it became the Koltonski Fire Station. Cancelled Oct.. 1, 1912. $5-6

Student Body at
Opening of New R.H.S. Field

1929

Rare black and white photo post card of the Student Body at Opening of New Rutland High School Field in 1929.
Condition "as is". $20

Rutland Vt.. High School. Cancelled Jan. 19, 1910. $5-6

High School Rutland, Vt.. Cancelled Mar 27, 1911. $5-6

High School, Rutland, Vt.. Made for N.J. Rowley, News dealer, Rutland, Vt..
Cancelled Oct.. 13, 1909. $7-8

Rutland High School, Rutland, Vt.. The old Rutland High School. Cancelled Jan. 31, 1905. $5-6

High School, Rutland, Vt.. Inscription on the back "Mrs. Leonard Cameron, Rutland, Vt.. 2-3-45" $5-6

Rutland, Vt.. Business College. In 1899 Mr. Liwelyn J. Egelston took over the Rutland English and Classical Institute, incorporating as Rutland Business College. At the time the college had state of the art equipment such as a letter press, Edison mimeograph and typewriters. At the beginning of the twentieth century there was a high demand for typists graduating from the Rutland Business College. Cancelled Aug.. 17, 1909. $7-8

State House of Correction, Rutland, Vt.

State House of Correction, Rutland, Vt.. Built in 1878 at the
corner of State Street and Pierpoint Avenue, below Pine Hill. $15

8

Institutions

Rutland Regional Medical Facility began on February 10, 1890 as a ten-bed hospital. Susan Pierpoint bequeathed all of her property to her sister, Julia, and stipulated that if she died with a will, the estate would be used to establish a hospital within five years or the Rutland Missionary Society would become the beneficiary. In 1891 the building site was chosen. After failed fundraising, the founders adopted Articles of Association and petitioned the Vermont Legislature for incorporation. The Rutland Hospital Association, the second hospital in Vermont, was incorporated on November 27, 1892. Rutland Hospital opened on September 6, 1896.

On October 4, 1956, groundbreaking began for a new, four-story, 155-bed hospital at the Chaffee Farm on Allen Street. The new building was dedicated on September 20, 1958 and patients moved in on October 4, 1958.

In January, 1983, the hospital's name was changed to Rutland Regional Medical Center. In 1985, Comprehensive Health Resources Inc. (CHRI), a holding company, was established. In 1998 CHRI's name was changed to Rutland Regional Health Services.

In 1986, a campaign began for the Rutland East building project, after which an addition, including the Community Cancer Center, was completed. Today, Rutland Regional Medical Center is Vermont's second-largest health care facility.

Rutland Mental Health Services and Rutland Community Programs are located at 78 South Main Street. The mission is to improve the overall quality of life for residents in the greater Rutland Region by offering an array of high-quality health, human services, education, employment and rehabilitative programs that empower individuals, families and communities to reach their full potential. The Community Care Network (CCN) is the parent corporation of Rutland Mental Health Services (RMHS) and Rutland Community Programs (RCP), RMHS was organized to maintain and

Open House

March 2, 2009
4:00-6:30 p.m.

Rutland Mental Health Services

During the 21st Century Rutland Mental Health Services expanded and consolidated their Community Access Program (CAP) at their 78 South Main Street, Rutland, Vt.. building. Program from their Open House on March 2, 2009. Overseen by a Board of Directors and managed by Dan Quinn the current President and CEO. $2-3

dear Cleora

We will start for

your place next

Tuesday on the seven

oclock train A. M.

if nothing happens

Miss Cleora Webb

Keeseville

N. Y.

Original black and white photo made into a
post card "Old Ladies Home, Rutland, Vt.."
Cancelled Jun. 15, 1910. $40

Old Ladie's Home, Rutland, Vt.

operate a community mental health and developmental disabilities system providing medical, clinical and supportive services, to promote health, and to further other benevolent, scientific and educational activities. RCP is organized exclusively for charitable, educational and scientific purposes including but not necessarily limited to the following purpose: to sponsor, develop, promote and conduct educational programs, social services and programs that are charitable, scientific or educational and that address the health needs of the community at large. The Community Care Network Substance Abuse Services was established to assist those[11] with a disease that affects the social, emotional, physical, mental and spiritual aspects of life. Rutland is also home to the Marble Valley Regional Correctional Facility, located at 167 State Street.

Rutland, Vt.., Hospital. Chartered in 1892. Built in 1895 on property on Nichols Street. $7-8

RUTLAND HOSPITAL, RUTLAND, VERMONT.

Rutland, Vt. Hospital.

Rutland Hospital, Rutland, Vermont showing the new addition added in 1909. Today Rutland Regional Medical Center a 188 bed hospital—with state of the art technology and world-class doctors, surgeons, nurses, and staff – is at Allen Street and Stratton Road. Visit www.rrmc.org Cancelled Sept.. 6, 1920. $3-4

MAIN STREET PARK,
RUTLAND, VT.

217014

Main Street Park, Rutland, Vt.. 19th Century photograph of the park at the intersection of West and Main Streets.
The old bandstand remains today. The park is the heart of community with events such as "Art in the Park." $3-4

9

Parks and Recreation

Rutland's Main Street Park contains the Green Mountain Boy Monument that honors Ethan Allen, one of the founding fathers of Vermont and leader of the Green Mountain Boys. The Green Mountain Boys were soldiers from Vermont who fought for independence in the American Revolution.

The Chaffee Art Center, at 16 South Main Street, annually presents two fine art and craft festivals called "Art In The Park" at the Main Street Park. Thousands of tourists swarm to enjoy these shows in August and October. Each features fine artists and crafts persons, musical entertainment and food, as well as special events for children. Art In The Park was declared one of "Vermont's Top Ten Events" by the Vermont Chamber of Commerce and was named as the "Sunshine Artist 200 Best" of shows held throughout North America.

Rutland Recreation and Parks runs a wide range of activities and facilities. They own and maintain playgrounds at Meadow Street, Madison Street, Temple Street, Rotary Field, White's Playground, Dana Recreational Center, Keefe Gym, Depot and Main Street Parks. Rutland has a 300-acre, "Pine Hill" park offering trials for mountain biking, hiking, and other outdoor recreation. At the park's entrance is the Flip Side Skate Park, municipally operated in an open-sided, closed-roof arena at the Giorgetti Ice Arena and Athletic Center. A non-profit volunteer organization named the Pine Hill Partnership formed to steward the 300 acre woods of Pine Hill Park. Through the cooperation of the Rutland Recreation Department, the organization has brought about the transformation

Handcolored.

The Common on South Main Street, Rutland, Vt.

The Common on South Main Street, Rutland, Vt.. $8-9

seen throughout the park. Partnering and coordinating with many local groups, individuals, businesses, schools and agencies, The Pine Hill Partnership has painstakingly formed the park's uniquely diverse and beautiful 16 mile trail system. (For further information visit www.rutlandrec.com, www.pinehillpark.org, and www.rutlandcreekpath.com)

Rutland Country Club, Rutland, Vermont. Cancelled Aug. 29, 1912. $5-6

STATUE IN HONOR OF THE GREEN MOUNTAIN BOYS, RUTLAND, VT.

Rutland Country Club, Rutland, Vt.. Cancelled July 6, 1908. $8-9

Statue in Honor of the Green Mountain Boys, Rutland, Vt.. Sent to Mrs. W. P. Abbott, 41 Union Street, Greenfield, MA from Nell D. Williams on holiday at Lake Bomoseen. Cancelled Aug. 10, 1917. $3-4

Rutland, Vt. Main St. Park.

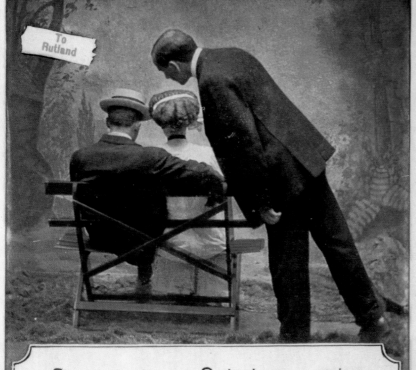

To Rutland

The people here in Rutland are so curious that no matter where you are they will not give you a minutes peace and quiet.

Rutland, Vt.. Main St. Park. "The people here in Rutland are so curious that no matter where you are they will not give you a minute's peace and quiet." Cancelled Sept.. 16, 1910. $15

Green Mountain Boy Monument, Rutland, Vt.. Post Card published by Rutland News Co., Rutland, Vt.. $5-6

GREEN MOUNTAIN. BOY MONUMENT. RUTLAND. VT.

61449

Rutland, Vt.. At the Golf Grounds. Formerly the farm of Colonel Redfield Proctor. $5-6

Municipal Swimming Pool, Rutland, Vt.. Built in 1929 swimmers enjoyed until 1974, demolished in 1977. In 1969 a new pool was constructed at the White Playground. The White Pool opened in 1970 and is the only 50 meter pool in the state. Cancelled Aug. 22, 1931. $4-5

The Rutland Country Club and Golf Course as seen from the 16th Green, Rutland, Vt.. Colonel Redfield Proctor kept pace with the twentieth century interest in the sport of golf. Note the clothes. $20

Aerial View of Rutland, Vermont, Rutland Fair in the foreground. Rutland second largest city in the State, is on U.S. Rt. 7 and U.S. Rt. 4. As a tourist center, it is convenient to all types of recreation, including bathing, fishing, golf, riding, hiking, and motor trips to many points of scenic attraction. Color by John B. Hustler. Pub. By Forward's Color Productions, Inc., Manchester, Vermont 05254. Addressed to Miss Catherine Young, 6313 West Halbert, Bethesda, Maryland, 20034. $4-5

Entrance to Fair Grounds, at Rutland Fair. Starts each year on Labor Day, Rutland, Vt.. The state fair is held here in Rutland along with many other activities through the year. $8-9

Municipal Swimming Pool, Rutland, Vt.—51

Municipal Swimming Pool, Rutland, Vt.. Fun events, lessons and lifeguard training all took place at the pool. $4-5

Rutland Fair, Sept.. 7-8-9-10-11 post card. Advertising post card. "The Rutland Fair is the event of the year in Vermont. It takes more than one day to see everything. The Free Carnival each evening is a wonder. You had better take it in!!" Front has photograph of Merchants Row, Rutland, Vt. $10

The best dressed men at the Fair wear the Famous Rochester "Clothes to Fit" by Nichols, the Clothier Headquarters in Rutland. Souvenir post card written on where it states: "Write below and tell your friends what a good time you are having at the fair." $10

Mountain Top (Inn) Club in the Green Mountains, 600 acre private estate on lake, 2000 feet altitude. All year around sports facilities. Chittenden (near Rutland) Vermont. Chittenden Reservoir is the body of water in the background. Cancelled Oct. 9, 1947

Dorr's Bridge and Otter Creek, showing Green Mountain Range. Rutland, Vt.

Dorr's Bridge and Otter Creek, showing Green Mountain Range, Rutland, Vt. This bridge extended to River Street over the Otter Creek to the ever growing Rutland City. The bridge was 120 feet in length and stood for 75 years. It was washed away during the flood of 1927. Cancelled Mar 2, 1910. $10

BILLINGS BRIDGE, RUTLAND, VT.

Billings Bridge, Rutland, Vt. Farmers haying. Photograph Post Card. $10

BIRD MOUNTAIN – NEAR RUTLAND, VERMONT

Bird Mountain – Near Rutland, Vermont. This is the site of the Traverse family farm. A family of loggers they logged the trees and then were given the land that has been farmed by the family since the 1920s. Currently farmed by Brian Traverse, niece Rachael (Traverse) Barbagallo is the assistant to this author. $7-8

Mount Hanley, Rutland, Vermont.

Mount Hanley, Rutland, Vermont. $7-8

Otter Creek and Dorr Bridge, Rutland, Vt. Note the house called "Fern Hill" home of William and Zulma DeLacy Dorr Steele. Cancelled Aug. 22, 1907 on the front, Aug. 21, 1907 on the back by the one cent stamp. $7-8

Rare black and white photo post card of Otter Creek, Rutland, Vt. St. Peter's Church, rectory and school in the background. Unknown fisherman in the foreground with the "Catch of the Day." $30

Clarendon Gorge, near Rutland, Vt. Cancelled Aug., 3 & Aug. 5, 1907. $7-8

Rutland, VT. Pine Hill Pond. $10

"O'er Hill and Dale" View of Mt. Killington early 20th Century. "Photostint" post card. $4-5

Rutland, Vermont. Drive along Lake Bomoseen. Lake Bomossen located in Castleton, VT approximately 12 miles from Rutland Downtown. $7-8

Tragedy

The Rutland State Fairgrounds is at 175 South Main Street (Route 7). In 1846 the Rutland Fair was a one-day event, with midway rides, entertainment shows, agricultural exhibits, livestock and a petting zoo. By 1859 it had grown into a week-long event and was moved to what has become the Vermont State Fairgrounds.

In September of 1913—the Wright brothers' first flight had been just ten years earlier—five hundred people crowded the fairgrounds in anticipation of the first air show in Vermont. George Schmitt, a Rutland citizen, was the scheduled pilot and fairgoers were excited to see their hometown son perform. He flew 130 miles the first day of the fair, carrying passengers on some of the flights. On the second day he carried mail from the fairgrounds to the local Rutland post office, and in the afternoon gave rides to fairgoers. At the end of the day, George was in the air with a passenger, Dyer Spellman, an Assistant Judge of the Municipal Court. The airplane engine stalled and, as the story goes, Dyer Spellman panicked, breaking essential wires as the plane crashed to the ground two hundred feet below. The plane's radiator landed on top of George Schmitt, crushing his skull, hip and jaw, resulting in his death four hours later at the Rutland Hospital. Unfortunately, at the age of twenty-one, George Schmitt made Vermont aviation history by being the first aviator killed in an airplane mishap.

By 1926 the Rutland Fair ranked among the top ten best state fairs in the United States. In 1972 the name was officially changed to the Vermont State Fair. Today, the Fair is ten days long and is held in September, with entertainment for everyone, including a demolition derby, Future Farmers of America show events, music and concerts by entertainers Wynonna Judd, Rick Springfield and Charlie Pride

Rutland has had its tragedies, snow storms, floods and fires, but this salt-of-the-earth community, rich in tradition, family values and "Support Vermont and Buy Local" ideology, has continued to flourish. With a "reconnecting for Rutland's future" strategic plan for the downtown, good community leaders and volunteers committed to ensuring the success of Rutland from the arts to agriculture, Rutland, Vermont, continues to thrive and remains one of the most beautiful and picturesque towns in the United States.

A one-acre area of land in downtown known as "the pit" slated for development in 2011. The new office building is planned to hold offices, education and civic space. At the intersection of Center and Wales Street this space was formally the site of the Berwick Hotel. In the 19th Century one of the grandest hotels, by the 20th Century the street level had shops to include the Steiner & Sons Piano store. Unfortunately a fire started on the upper floors known as the "Town House" and the Berwick burned to the ground in 1973. Today the Berwick site is considered a site that will reconnect Rutland with the future.

Aviator Geo. Schmitt killed at Rutland Vt. Sept 2 1i9I3.

Aviator George Schmitt killed at Rutland Vt.. Sept. 2, 1913. During the Rutland Fair Grounds Aviation Meet – at the age of twenty-one - George Schmitt was the first aviation death in Vermont's history. A very rare black and white photo post card of George and his plane the "Red Devil" at Wilson Field, Rutland. $150

"George Schmitt's wrecked aero plane, with which he was killed. Sept. 2, 1913 (Charles A.) Hayles, Photo." On Sept.. 2, 1913 at the State Fairgrounds, Rutland, Vermont—to the horror of the 500 spectators below—George's plane stopped, turned and fell 200 feet to the ground. Passenger J. Dyer Spellman, Asst. Judge of the Municipal Court thought to be the cause of the crash: "He lost his head." Spellman was badly burned but survived. $150

Geo. Schmitt's wrecked Aeroplane, with which he was killed. Sept. 2, 1913. Hayles, Photo.

Index